THE GEMS I PICKED UP

Sharing Insights I Have Picked Up Along My Recovery Journey

Michael Cabriel Kintu Kayondo

Independent

Copyright © 2024 Michael Gabriel Kintu Kayondo

All rights reserved

Scriptures taken from the Holy Bible, New International Version®, NIV®. Copyright © 1973, 1978, 1984, 2011 by Biblica, Inc.™ Used by permission of Zondervan. All rights reserved worldwide. www.zondervan.com The "NIV" and "New International Version" are trademarks registered in the United States Patent and Trademark Office by Biblica, Inc.™

Scripture quotations taken from the Amplified® Bible (AMPC),

Copyright © 1954, 1958, 1962, 1964, 1965, 1987 by The Lockman Foundation

Used by permission. lockman.org

No part of this book may be reproduced, or stored in a retrieval system, or transmitted in any form or by any means, electronic, mechanical, photocopying, recording, or otherwise, without express written permission of the publisher.

ISBN-13:

Cover design by: Art Painter

Library of Congress Control Number: 2018675309

Printed in the United States of America

I dedicate this book to all those in recovery.

Table of Contents

WHAT TO DO DIFFERENTLY 1

UNBELIEF: 5

ABOUT HONESTY: 7

WHAT I DO TO STAY SOBER: 11

SELF-TALK: 13

MORE ABOUT RELATIONSHIPS: 17

OWNING UP: 23

DEALING WITH ANXIETY AND DEPRESSION: 27

MANAGING TRIGGERS: 32

ABOUT ESCAPES: 36

ABOUT BEING DESPERATE: 40

DOING THE GOOD I OUGHT TO DO: 46

ADDRESSING ADDICTION AT THE WORKPLACE: 48

TOOLS OF OVERCOMING ADDICTION: 53

ABOUT CONFIDENTIALITY: 57

ABOUT EX-LOVERS: 61

ABOUT THE AUTHOR 66

WHAT TO DO DIFFERENTLY

Well, we can talk about what we can do differently or do better to maintain our sobriety and walk stronger in our recovery.

• Pray more and root your prayer in surrender. Honest truth be told, you cannot do most of these things in your own power. As you pray more, with prayer rooted in surrender, more grace is given. I've got to see a different face of grace and that's insight. With grace comes deeper insight into what's against you. The deeper the insight you get, the more grateful you are and thankful for God's mercy.

You cannot stay sober in your own power. You need grace. Be more vulnerable with God. Express your weaknesses to Him genuinely and ask Him to be your strength. Will, self and all these mind power things that are being pushed are very powerless when it comes to keeping sober. Only the grace of God can keep you sober. Pray for it.

• Extend your knowledge base. Knowledge is power. Read more. And not just any kind of reading, inspired reading. The thing with inspired reading is that the words you read are activated and are life. They are daily bread for the soul. This life from activated words (revelation) gives hope to your soul and comfort and peace.

Read something you are led to or inspired to read. In the psychology field, you can study much about self-esteem, coping mechanisms, Freudian slips and so much more. Read something that will help you shine a light into yourself. Shining a light into the understanding that you couldn't have done any better with the tools you had then. This uplifts the unnecessary burden of regret from our hearts.

I haven't yet come across a book that has so much life-giving power like the Bible which feeds our souls with hope. When the Words in it are activated by the Spirit, there's much life that is sourced from those words.

- Determine to find that peace within. A lot of times, we tell ourselves that we will feel peaceful when we have this or that. A peace that comes from without is never lasting, but a peace that comes from within is eternal. Work has to be put in to find peace within. The 12 Steps gives us the action steps we can take to find that peace within.

- Be more around like minds. There's something about being around like minds. There's a power that rubs off from them to you. You are the average of those you fellowship with. Fellowship is deep brotherhood and sisterhood that rooted in vulnerability, honesty and genuine support. Seek out like minds that you can be around more this year.

Being around like minds will help you to trust again. It will help you to love again and most of all, it will help you to see yourself in a better light that you are valued, you are loved and not just tolerated but celebrated.

- Give more. One thing I learnt is you can never out give God. Give more of your time if you have reservations when it comes to money. People are very reserved when it comes to giving money because they have been taken advantage of, lied to and taken for granted. I felt that same way but when I started giving to God; not worrying about if those I've given to have taken me for a ride and building resentment (my heart being in the right place), I started getting a lot more from my giving. A person who gives genuinely benefits more from his or her giving. When your giving is genuine (doesn't expect anything in return), you get much more.

- Make plans that are not set in stone. Leave room for flexibility. Be like water that always adapts to the shape of the vessel it's in. Have a daily routine you maintain but always leave room for the inevitable.

- Determine to be exceedingly honest. People that heal extremely fast are that are honest. When you are honest, you may not see the results immediately but honesty lays a very firm foundation that bears the weight of the insight, wisdom, depth and hope among others that inevitably come your way and usher you into your healing. Hope breaks a dishonest person. For instance, if a dishonest person gets a lot of money at once, he will hit many walls and make many losses. But when an honest person gets money, they will benefit greatly from it. These virtues are similar and only a heart that is pure and genuine can bear the weight of them.

• Be more thankful. Don't regret your bad luck. What you term as bad luck could be redemption from worse luck. God has a way of sustaining us through wilderness experiences that we perceive as harsh in the moment but as time reveals more, we see that He saved us from worse that could've happened.

• Lastly, don't worry. We fear much when we determine to do right or when we set our feet in the path of the right direction. We think about the many things that can possibly go wrong but worry not, no one can snatch you out of His hands. Nothing can sabotage your progress on the path of healing, growth and recovery for He is with you. The only things that might sabotage (that's how we see it) our progress are those things He permits that we might pick up lessons from them.

John 10:27-29 NIV

My sheep listen to my voice; I know them, and they follow me. I give them eternal life, and they shall never perish; no one will snatch them out of my hand. My Father, who has given them to me, is greater than all; no one can snatch them out of my Father's hand.

UNBELIEF:

I have got to see that the greatest sin is unbelief.

Unbelief opens a door to many other sins.

Unbelief that you are not worthy of marriage will open a door to looseness.

Unbelief that God cannot meet your needs will open a door to manipulation and control, plus greed. Get all you can and hoard it.

Unbelief will open a door to jealousy and envy when you see someone entering their own. In view of the fact that you don't believe you can enter your own, you hate on them.

Unbelief will open a door to betrayals and conspiracies to get them out of the way because you think you can't do it when they are still there.

Unbelief will make you put on masks, pretending much because you think people might think of you different when you show who you truly are.

One thing I've seen is that people respect real people.

Unbelief opens a door to pride and prayerlessness.

Unbelief that you can't live a full life sober empties all hope that one can indeed be sober.

Belief does the exact opposite. You will give of yourself more without fear, without reservations.

You will wait on God to make things happens trusting fully in His Word. Jeroboam was given many promises, but his unbelief got in the way.

Abraham too was given promises, belief got him to even almost sacrifice his son.

Sobriety and recovery have much to do with starting to believe.

ABOUT HONESTY:

Honesty is essential in recovery. Most people that struggle with overcoming addiction have issues with being honest.

For a person to heal and grow, they must become totally honest without reservations.

When a person wants to truly recover, they have to grow in honesty. The thing that hinders people from absolute sobriety is honesty. Lying is the conventional way of doing things. A friend that I highly regard and respect retorted to me once that, "sometimes, you have to lie to get by."

This might work for most things like business, for many of the second-hand things on the market are stolen things. From shoes to gadgets. There's a very big network of dishonest people who steal and lie.

To be honest means going against the status quo. It means that when you withdraw a sum of money from an agent who gives you much more by accident, you return the extra given. To be maintain sobriety, one has to be very straight in all their ways or a relapse is inevitable. A person that relapses over and over again has issues with being honest.

At the root of addiction lies some form of deception. Deception can express itself outwardly when a person acts deceptively or it can express itself inwardly when a person believes and entertains deceptive things. Honesty is the antidote to that.

To stay sober absolutely, that is to say, without any crutches, one needs to get really honest. I'm going to talk about how we can grow in honesty in our day to day lives.

We are human and we all make mistakes. The thing that sets you above that flaw of humanity is what you do after you make the mistake.

For some of us that truly want to recover, we may find that we may have to leave our dishonest jobs or drop the dishonest way of getting or making money. That indirectly compromises our recovery. There are many dishonest things we do that indirectly compromise our recovery.

A person in recovery who is hitting on and lying to many compromises their recovery.

A person who lies to get by compromises their recovery.

A person who runs away from debtors and doesn't pay debts, even when he or she has the money indirectly compromises their recovery.

A person who steals (I recently learnt there's a legal way of stealing) compromises their recovery.

A person involved in any trade or skill that profits from deception indirectly compromises their recovery.

It is hard for people who are involved in deception to maintain lasting sobriety. Lawyers that win cases with the awareness that their client is guilty indirectly compromise their recovery. Their professional lives may grow but their personal lives will depreciate.

Many survive online by catfishing or flirting indirectly compromise their recovery.

A person who does not keep their word or honors it indirectly compromises their recovery.

By indirectly compromising one's recovery, I mean, opening up doors wide to negative emotions like guilt and regret to flow in that inevitably leads to relapse.

Here are some of the ways a person can grow in honesty.

- **Stop running away from debtors.** Make a list of all those whose debts you have and reach out to them, showing them your willingness to pay. Most times, you may not have the money to pay but show them your willingness to pay. Don't hide from them. When God sees that your heart is in the right place and is not fearful or deceptive, He makes a way for you to pay all your debts.

- **Identify all avenues where lies have been told and close them.** For some, it might mean closing social media accounts, for others, it might mean stopping to reach out to people in deceptive ways.

- **Make amends for every lie told.** This might mean calling up and meeting those you have lied to and telling them what's up. I'm very fortunate that my list was not very long but I had to go through each and every one I lied to to make those amends. This made me feel like a fool initially but later the reward of it was more than I could ever imagine; the peace and the relief.

Doing the next right thing on our journey of recovery will make us feel like fools, but at the end of the day, these right steps we take have untold rewards.

Reading the Chapter, "Into Action," of the Big Book will throw more light on being honest. It pays to be honest.

- **Pray for the grace to be honest**. Many times, we find ourselves in situations where we have to tell lies to get by. This reveals little grace to be honest. When you pray for more grace to be honest, you will find that you don't have to lie to get by no more.

- **Be more open and vulnerable in your communication.** Again, this will make you look and feel like a fool. People might take it as being weak but the peace of mind you will get from doing this surpasses understanding. It's very relieving where you don't always have to keep scripts in your head and play them out whenever. When a person is honest, they will always stay consistent in what they say regardless of the passing of time.

WHAT I DO TO STAY SOBER:

Here are some tips that have helped me stay sober.

- God (Jesus) gets all the credit. He has upheld my hand in places where I would slip and fall that I never fall even in the most tempting of places.

- I'm very persistent and persevering to get closure in situations where guilt and bad emotions would arise. Where I've gone wrong, I'm quick to make right at any cost. At times that cost is patience and time. I leave no room for guilt and shame to cloud my sobriety.

- I don't allow things to eat me up. I either write about it and post or tell someone. I share my vulnerability out there and my weaknesses. I'm not afraid to. I don't pretend to be strong in some areas, yet I'm not. I'm strong in some areas. That strength is undisputed.

- I value my alone time. A man can bear anything that comes his way once he finds meaning in it. Spending time alone has helped me to find meaning in life, to swim in its depth. I am not moved by much. I tried looking outside for meaning, it was vain. Now I look within.

Spending time alone has given me the opportunity to see, to appreciate the beauty I have within me. My stones are set in antimony. I was dwelling deeply on the ugliness within, as well as following up with destructive action. Now I see beauty. You can never destroy something you love.

- I'm passionate about helping the next. At times I'm misunderstood or taken out of context. I never worry about that. The thing that levels it up is; my heart is in the right place. Service floods my heart with peace.

SELF-TALK:

Today, we will talk about the things we tell ourselves that work against our recovery.

The self-talk we have, when no one is with you. It can be outright or just in your mind.

There's an abundance of things we tell ourselves that hinder us from staying sober. We tell things to ourselves most especially when alone or when we find someone we can trust and be vulnerable with.

When a person is used to being effective when under the influence (artists getting drunk before they perform, doctors numbing themselves as they work, long distance drivers using stimulants to be alert), that person tells or asks himself if it will be possible to be effective and deliver at their jobs when sober.

"Is it possible to do what I do sober?" "Can I pull it off when not under the influence?" The internal monologue goes on to say no, and the mind has a way of working with what you give it, raking up all the evidence that supports what you give it.

The mind will remind you when you pulled it off so well and mention that you pulled it off under the influence. This leads to justification of the use or the drink and eventually, you drink or use. What started it in motion? The unbelief that you couldn't pull it off when sober.

Negative self-talk comes up at times when it comes to intimacy. There are those that cannot enjoy sex sober. They have to be under the influence.

Either to numb feelings of being taken advantage of, or to silence the voice of conviction, telling them that what they are doing is wrong (this happens commonly with forbidden sex).

The internal monologue goes like, "it will not be possible to enjoy myself sober." This builds into drinking or using before meeting up with the person.

Reason why it's very important to abstain from sex, most especially in the initial stages of one's recovery.

There are also things we tell ourselves when we are overwhelmed by intense emotion. We tell ourselves that maybe we deserved it when we are betrayed. We feel we don't deserve loyalty. We tell ourselves that maybe we are not worth it when we are let down. Feelings of unworthiness clothe our souls.

It is this self-talk that either builds us if positive or breaks us if negative. "Will I be able to pass through this without getting high?" Some of us have so much anxiety in meeting people. "Will I be able to be calm when I meet so and so?"

And the mind tells you, probably not. If we are honest with ourselves, we will identify that relapses or slips back into unhealthy behaviors or patterns are always preceded by negative self-talk where we cannot affirm positive possibilities

There are situations that overwhelm us and we don't pause to kindle our faith. Just as much as a person can go through anything while high, a person can go through anything while sober. There's the other side of the coin of possibilities we don't look at.

A belief is impressed upon people who have jobs which handle a lot of traffic that they cannot do what they do unless they are under the influence.

For instance, those in the media, those in catering, those in hospitals.

Many use stimulants instead of depressants. These are not easy to detect because a person stays in control of themselves but their energy levels are up.

What you tell yourself, the internal monologue you have has a lot to do with whether you stay sober or you relapse. Many, when they come out of rehab, they spend days, weeks and months telling themselves that they will not be able to handle being out there on their own. Eventually, they relapse.

They have been building it up without realizing it.

How can we better our self-talk that we may stay sober?

Like all things in recovery, most of the work has to be done by you. Start observing situations or events in your life where negative self-talk comes up and analyze it. Could that event or situation have triggered a wound that was not yet healed? Could it have brought to the surface unhealed pain?

As you analyze those situations or events, forgive and come up with positive affirmations to counter the negative self-talk you have been having. In the beginning, it may seem as if you are making progress but keep on. After a while, much of the negative self-talk and the negative emotions it carries along with it will be scooped out of your thinking process.

MORE ABOUT RELATIONSHIPS:

I'm inspired to talk about being in a relationship or being in relationships.

Awareness is the deep understanding that you have no business being in a relationship until you have availed yourself to your healing.

With a recognition and appreciation of your pain, you keep away from certain things and situations until you are healed. An intimate relationship being the foremost.

Or else, drama (codependency) always arises.

Some are fortunate that when their relationships fail, they sit back and give themselves time to heal (these are the wise ones) and others are unfortunate that they move quickly into new relationships which end up being worse than the ones they were in.

The cycle worsens if you don't sit back and give yourself time to heal. It never gets better. The new person you meet might be better, but codependency is already set into motion since you haven't done the work on you to heal.

Most times, those in codependent relationships struggle with substance abuse.

When it ends and you are aware that you have a background of pain, be very thankful and sit back, stay single for a while and work on you.

The mistake most of us make is going into relationships — most times it's due to the strong pull of intimacy — before we avail ourselves to healing.

The thing I have observed most, is that we enter into relationships with a baggage of survival skills we got while learning how to cope with the trauma we experienced. This can work out at times if the both parties are willing to put in the work to heal and grow. They never work out if only one party is putting in the effort.

The survival skill that breaks relationships the most is dishonesty (lies, deception, secrecy which the Baganda call okukukuta).

Here are insights to help in our healing when it comes to relationships, to determine whether we are ready or not to be in one.

The more the pain and trauma a person has gone through, the less the self-esteem they have, and the more the toxic defense mechanisms and unhealthy survival skills they have. I'm going to list some things that might shine some light into why, if you are in a relationship, it's not working out, or if you have broken up, why it never worked out.

Only children rarely have success in their relationships. Why? Because they are not heard, silenced by the too much noise coming from the unrealistic expectations of their parents. On the outside, it may look as if the parents are spoiling them but that is not it. What happens is that there's an abundance of material and a lack of emotional support in their lives. This is traumatic.

Only boy among girl siblings and only girl among boy siblings also fall under this. Rebellion, promiscuity, indiscipline are some of the things they do to cope with the pain in their lives. They will live lives craving for attention. Some get very famous but at the end of the day they can never have a healthy intimate relationship because it will be clouded by drama (codependency).

Those that were raised by single parents, or one parent left. In as much as the parent that stayed does all they can, the child/ren will always struggle with abandonment. The defense mechanism that pops up much in those who have feelings of abandonment is lying. And they easily fall prey to those that use them or control them (due to their low self-esteem).

A person who suffers abandonment will have accountability, trust and commitment issues. Ladies that suffer with abandonment sleep around much and guys too. It is impossible to do right by a person who has the hurt of abandonment.

Your best can never match up to heal the hurt. The only person that can heal that hurt is the person who is feeling the pain. They have to put in the work to heal. I know, regret clothes our souls when we think we could have done more. You couldn't do more. It's that person who suffered the hurt that could've done more.

People that are highly gifted, or are beautiful or are a minority, or are "different" from others in a way suffer trauma. If they don't do the work on themselves to heal, they in most cases are in or initiate unhealthy relationships. Intimacy brings out our latent pain like nothing else can. It's not that person that hurt you. It is your unhealed pain that hurt you. Even if you move on to the next, this unhealed pain comes out stronger and, in most cases, the relationship is worse.

There are some settings that are tolerated among us but are toxic and unhealthy. Growing up in a polygamous setting is the norm here. Polygamy opens many doors to rivalry, unhealthy competition, favoritism, secret envy and hatred, selfish ambition and conspiracies. All this is traumatic for everyone in that setting. A person from the kind of setting can rarely have or maintain a healthy intimate relationship.

There are more instances and situations in a person's life that open doors to intense trauma, which when unhealed, always turn toxic in one way or another in intimate relationships. We have heard many cases of people who are so good when you meet them but their mates tell you different. That is unhealed pain.

So how do you heal this pain? In all situations, whether you are in a codependent relationship, or you have left one or you are planning to enter into one with the naivety that it can turn codependent, you have to determine to put in the work to avail yourself to your healing.

How do you put in this work? Admission of powerlessness. That you cannot love right unless you heal. This will not only give you the strength to stay away because you deeply understand that hurting and being hurt is inevitable in such cases.

This admission of powerlessness will guide your actions. Where you gave money to win approval of your mate — this might be on a conscious or subconscious level — you stop because you get the awareness that no matter how much you give them time, money and devotion, it never fills. Why? Because the emptiness is in you, not them.

Abstinence is necessary in the healing process. Sportsmen that have got injuries are told to abstain for a certain period to heal. Abstinence is not only great for the healing of the body but also the mind and emotions.

Once the physical abstinence is realized, then a person who is determined to heal must take the next step to abstain emotionally.

Putting a stop to leading on those you could possibly want to be intimate with. Putting a stop to flirting, watching porn and being loose mentally.

These are some of the things you can do on the outside to heal as you do work too behind the scenes in growing your spiritual life; praying more, purifying your character with the 3 H's. That is growing in Hope, Humility and Honesty and availing yourself, surrendering yourself more to the Potter to mold you.

Working on your self-esteem. Identifying which instances where your self-esteem was chipped away. This is easy to do when you let your feelings guide you. How did you feel when so and so said this about you? Did you feel angry? Explore these emotions deeper. Below the anger, there is an undercurrent of rejection or abandonment.

Then also setting boundaries. Healthy boundaries. Smart boundaries. A lady that was abused will fear men and she might set a boundary of not visiting men at their places, but if that boundary is not smart or healthy; that is to say, if she keeps flirting with men and leading them on, chances are very high that she might be abused again in another setting.

Smart and healthy boundaries protect and have no leaks.

OWNING UP:

This is about owning up. To heal, one has got own up. Take responsibility.

There are many things we are passive about, for example, resentments. When you let it hurt and that hurt leads you to doing something destructive, you are not owning up.

We find in recovery, we have to do a little more owning up than those who have never struggled with addiction. When a person genuinely wants to recover, they will do all it takes to recover. That means going the extra mile, we have to over-perform ourselves and go above and beyond.

Doing an inventory, a fearless and searching moral inventory of ourselves sets us onto the path of owning up. You start seeing clearly where you were at fault, or where you missed the mark, or where you were passive when you could've done something.

Much happens to us when we don't do the work on ourselves. For instance, when we don't set healthy boundaries, we can host friends at our place when we are fully aware that they drink or smoke. When something happens and we relapse, we tend to blame our friends and not ourselves initially in our recovery.

A person that's owning up would not blame his friends or himself. He would look back and analyze where he or she opened the door, and forgive himself or herself for not knowing any better, forgive his friends and grow from that.

Owning up to me means identifying the doors we consciously or unconsciously open to the negative forces that surround us, then doing something to close them and purge ourselves of the negative.

As we grow spiritually, we discover we have power over immeasurably more than we previously thought. We have no power over what happens to us but we have power over how we feel about it. We have power over our thoughts, feelings and attitudes.

Owning up means pointing all the five fingers to ourselves with none pointed to others. The best of those out there say that we ought to point four fingers at ourselves and one to the world. When it comes to us in recovery, we go further; we point all our fingers to ourselves.

When someone in your life is a trigger, owning up would mean going deeper than focusing on the outer layers of it. A smart person in recovery would quickly note they haven't forgiven that person and are still harboring resentments towards that person.

When someone is still a trigger, it will reveal that you haven't yet worked on setting up healthy boundaries. True recovery means going to all places where free men go and socializing with whoever free people interact and socialize with.

When someone is still a trigger- I know some will mention that their landlords are triggers- that shows loops in your honesty and reveals that some work still has to be done in making amends.

The feelings we have towards something always attracts people who are at that same level of vibration towards us. When you feel bad about something, let's say a man, or a woman, you will open up doors within you and embrace unhealthy views and perspectives about women or men, and weirdly, the right men and women will always elude you. A person who understands owning up will note that by harboring these resentments, they never get to attract the right people.

Resentments build early on in our lives and are directly connected to the way we feel about our fathers- the primary man in our lives or our mothers the primary women in our lives. A person still having unworked on resentments against either the mother or the father will pass through life hitting walls in relationships, always blaming the other for all the things going wrong.

Owning up has a lot to do with identifying the doors we opened within us (the negative way we feel about certain things, situations and people) that grow subtly into unhealthy patterns and behaviors which ultimately fuel addiction in time. Recovery is all about you, so take charge and own up.

A person that's growing in recovery understands that not increasing his spiritual life will ultimately lead to a relapse. I see a lot of hope for a person who owns up and says, "I relapsed because I wasn't praying much." "I relapsed because I lied to so and so and opened up a door to guilt." There's so much hope in that person's recovery because they are truly owning up.

But when someone tells me that they relapsed because someone triggered them, I still see hope, but I also see relapse ahead until they can get to owning up and then doing the work.

Owning up is asking yourself always, "where did I go wrong, where did I

miss the mark, what didn't I do?" True owning up is asking yourself all this

WITHOUT CONDEMNING YOURSELF!

Self-condemnation shuts many doors of discovering who you are and your power.

In getting and growing to know who you are, you grow in owning up, and from this, eternal healing and life springs. The person who slaps another actually slaps himself. A deep understanding of owning up will show you this clearly. Jesus was telling us not to slap ourselves when you look at it in that context.

DEALING WITH ANXIETY AND DEPRESSION:

Today, we will talk about alcohol and drugs as a coping mechanism for depression and anxiety.

To better understand why alcohol is a drug of choice for many is to understand what alcohol is.

Alcohol is both a stimulant and a depressant. It's a stimulant when it first gets ingested into the system, then as more and more of it is taken in, it becomes a depressant.

You can see someone who has just started drinking get excited, get hyper and are energetic but as that person goes on drinking, their speech starts to slur, and their movements slow down. The excitement in the beginning is due to the stimulating effects of alcohol and the slowness in the end is due to the depressing effects of alcohol.

When a person is feeling low, the stimulating effect of alcohol works and when a person is hyper or anxious, the depressing or calming effect of alcohol works.

The thing about an alcoholic is that, whenever they are feeling low, they don't know how to stop at that stimulating effect of alcohol. They drink past it and tap into the depressing effect of alcohol. Non-alcoholics know when to stop but alcoholics don't.

Alcohol, being what it is explains why most people run to it as an escape. The best way to cope with stormy swings of mood that sway from anxiety to depression is to integrate healthy coping mechanisms, instead of drinking.

For most, alcohol raises them up when they are down and it brings them down when they are up, for instance when they are anxious, or when they are overly excited. This explains why when someone hits a jackpot, they celebrate it by drinking. The excitement is much.

People who use narcotics are well versed with manipulating stimulants and depressants to steady their mood. Cocaine stimulates, then they need a depressant like alcohol or heroin to level up their mood.

Webster's defines anxiety as an overwhelming sense of apprehension and fear often marked by physiological signs (such as sweating, tension, and increased pulse), by doubt concerning the reality and nature of the threat and by self-doubt about one's capacity to cope with it. Anxiety puts us in flight mode.

What are some healthy coping mechanisms that we can integrate that help either when we are anxious, or when we are depressed?

We can lessen our anxiety in three dimensions. Physically, emotionally and spiritually. Physically, we can improve our lifestyle- less sugar, less caffeine, more exercise and so on. There's much information out there in improving lifestyle.

You can go deeper in understanding your blood group. At times what we eat is in conflict with our blood. Going deeper into understanding your blood helps.

On the emotional, it has more to do with things that threaten your security. People that experienced abandonment, rejection, abuse are vulnerable to anxiety. And this anxiety is triggered whenever they face those things again or are in situations that trigger those past wounds. When something threatens our security, in this case, emotional security, we get anxious.

Tracing the trauma points in our lives and facing them helps us hit at the root where the flight mode initially entered our lives. When we start to face these lions, we find that we don't have to run anymore.

On the spiritual, we have to work toward living pure. The Bible says that the righteous are as bold as a lion. When you are living pure in all your ways, you will fear nothing. If you don't fear nothing, there's no need to run. Forgiveness, letting go, making amends, surrendering to God, severing all unhealthy attachments, drawing healthy boundaries ... all help deal with anxiety.

Owing no man nothing but a debt to love also helps. Growing in service fills this.

Depression is a state of feeling sad. This sadness can go low to despair and feeling unworthy. It has the potential to grow into schizophrenia, where the mind shuts down totally not to face reality. Some schizophrenic people gave up totally at some points in their lives. Something happened that made them lose hope.

Again, we can find ways to deal with this in three dimensions. We can deal with depression physically. Sometimes, an imbalance of neurotransmitters in the brain causes this. Psychiatry may come in handy in this, but depression is best handled in all dimensions.

Physically, we can find ways to up our mood without looking for an escape. Sugar and caffeine are very good to start with initially when a person gets sober. As time goes on, a person has to integrate healthy ways to get that kick. Exercise is great when it comes to this. A healthy diet too. One thing to note is, don't depend on something outside you to get the kick. That is temporary. What is eternal is, look for something within.

Emotionally, there are ways too to deal with depression. Maybe not making that amend is depressing you. Analyze what is depressing you and pierce through the layers of depression.

Spiritually, being grateful, singing more will help.

It's God's will for us to be happy. Sometimes you have to come against these feelings in prayer (Address Depression and Anxiety with Psalms 35). Growing in prayer tremendously. There are instances where a person has tried everything in the book but still hits walls or the depression intensifies. Growing in the skill of prayer helps.

People like us are very persistent in finding solutions and in most cases, we turn the world upside down to find solutions in vain. We resent the one who could give us a lasting solution. That is God. We resent Him for abandoning us according to our perception, we resent Him for letting some things happen to us. We never try to look for a solution in Him.

Growing in spirit, we get to see that God is Love. The negative forces in the world are to blame. For if it wasn't for God, it could've been worse. Instead of blaming God, blame the negative more and grow in thanksgiving towards God. When you embrace this, you will find that you have mastery over feelings of anxiety and depression. This grows on you as you don't pass the blame to the wrong Person.

As you thank God more for standing by you and not abandoning you, He will reveal more to you and show you situations where He stepped in and saved you. We direct our anger and bitterness to Someone who has been with us through it all.

Mastery over depression and anxiety is got when we come against the negative in the world with Father's power. And that is by fully embracing the truth that He means us no harm and that He can never leave us nor forsake us.

MANAGING TRIGGERS:

This is about managing and avoiding triggers.

How do we manage and avoid triggers?

Triggers are people, situations and things that prod unhealed wounds in us, resurrecting the pain we felt then into now and in some cases, we run to substances or unhealthy behaviors (relapse) to cope.

How do we avoid triggers? In today's world, it's getting harder and harder to avoid some triggers. There are two kinds of separation that I'm going to talk about that might be relevant to our discussion today. They are used mostly in Christian circles but can also be used in this context.

There's a separation from the world. This means avoiding all tempting places. Avoiding bars, avoiding watching TV because you might see alcohol ads. Avoiding parties ... This works for a short time as the temptation always finds you in places where you hide to run away from it.

Then there's a separation unto God, or in this case, sobriety or recovery. You can be anywhere, go where free men go, even at times in bars but due to the reason that you are separated unto God (have a change of heart from an alcoholic one to one that can't be moved by temptation), you don't drink.

So how do we grow to manage (be unmoved) triggers that are all around us? How does a person who has a history of addiction comfortably store beers in his fridge that are kept for his nonalcoholic friends he hosts once in a while?

How do you get to that? The answer is in having a change of heart- from an alcoholic one to a healed heart (a heart that doesn't desire to self-destruct, or run to substances and unhealthy behaviors to cope) no more.

The first step is dealing with resentment. A friend explained to me that resentments are hurts that we play over and again in our minds. How could he do this to me? How could he belittle me like that? How could they strip me bare like that? When we play these hurtful memories over and over again in our minds, the build into resentments.

This is self-triggering. Even when alone, you find yourself running to a drink or engaging in unhealthy behaviors because these hurts replay over and over again in the person's mind.

This explains the paradox why some people say that so and so was in a very good environment, had the best opportunities …, there's no reason why he or she could end up like that. There is a very strong reason- that person was playing their pain over and over again in their minds.

Resentments is the pain one replays over and over again. What helps here is forgiveness of self. There's something going on in today's world where we know that it's very toxic to judge another. But have you ever asked yourself how many people are walking around having passed judgement on themselves? Self-condemnation? Many of us passed judgement on ourselves. Forgiveness of self helps in this.

Step 5 works miracles in this. - Admitted to God, to ourselves, and to another human being the exact nature of our wrongs. In doing this step, portals to forgiveness are opened and assurance that God forgives you blankets you. There's no reason to pass judgement on yourself.

That you may not be a self-trigger.

Secondly, forgiving others genuinely comes in handy when it comes to managing triggers. When you forgive genuinely, someone that agitated you in the past won't be able to do it anymore. Forgiveness strips whoever treated you "unjustly" of their power over you.

Forgiveness levels the ground when it comes to people triggering us. The more you forgive, the less people have power over you to agitate you. Growing in forgiveness is key.

Another way of managing triggers is drawing healthy boundaries. A hospital has an intensive care unit where the critically ill are put, it has a general ward where those who need to be monitored are put and it also has an outpatient department where those whose cases that don't need admission go.

Drawing healthy boundaries comes in handy here. Not everyone has access to someone in ICU, not even the family members. In recovery, knowing where you are is very important. Some are in ICU but are carrying on like they are in outpatient.

Knowing where you are in recovery is key. This knowledge grows with acceptance. For some, when they are new to recovery, having a phone is a trigger. They are in "ICU." When a person knows where they are at in recovery, walking away from certain triggering situations becomes easy.

The more critical you are, the tougher the boundaries you have to set.

Growing spiritually indirectly helps us manage triggers. Spirituality to me is 3 H's. Growing in Honesty, Humility and Hope will help create a path for you in a wilderness of triggers.

Pride, Dishonesty and Despair are some of the reasons why people relapse.

ABOUT ESCAPES:

Let's talk about Escapes. To me, escapes mean things that we do to ease our discomfort in certain situations we might be in for example, when we are bored or lonely.

In recovery, when we find healing, sobriety and growth, discomfort is dealt with. We start doing things because we love to do them, because we want to do them …, not because we are pushed into doing them by the discomfort that's prodding us.

Merriam-Webster dictionary defines escapism as a "habitual diversion of the mind to purely imaginative activity or entertainment as an escape from reality or routine."

A Google definition of escapism is "the tendency to seek distraction and relief from unpleasant realities, especially by seeking entertainment or engaging in fantasy."

"Virtual reality offers a form of escapism."

Escapes are those things we run to either consciously or they are wired into our systems that we unconsciously run to, to ease our discomfort in certain situations. Only to feel empty and unsatisfied after.

The most tolerated escape is caffeine. This is either in coffee or tea or soft drinks. You will observe that most who complain about being "stressed" always run to caffeine. A cup of coffee or tea is a good pass time, a good way to get back that physical motivation. It always comes at a cost though.

When the effects wear off, the energy levels at the lowest.

Another escape that people use is "work." To avoid facing some things, a person will say that they are always "busy." This goes hand in hand with avoidance. A busy person will always create time for important things.

Why? Because they always have their priorities set in the right order. Someone telling you that they are always "busy" is a red flag.

Binges on series, movies and the obvious ones when it comes to drinking are escapes. A person will want out of reality for a while, so they binge on something to ease the discomfort.

Codependent relationships are escapes. The thing about escapes is that you deeply know that they are vain but you engage in them anyway. It's a kind of suspended reality they put a person into, where they don't have to face themselves or find solutions.

In codependency, either playing the savior or the victim is an escape. The savior derives his sense of meaning for "being there" for the other and the victim derives their sense of meaning from blaming the savior. That mind state is an escape.

Social media is an escape for most. Where we scroll endlessly to pass time or with the hope that we will land on something that will miraculously set us free or make us feel better about ourselves.

Sleeping around or masturbating or engaging in any sexual perversion are escapes. There are some things related to our sexuality that we don't want to face. They might be repressed memories, or a trauma that hurt us deeply that we don't want to remember.

This also includes watching porn.

Having moments of fantasizing or daydreaming are also escapes. Some have even set aside time to daydream by calling it meditation.

The greatest escape for us when it comes to recovery is denial. Where we don't want to admit that we have a problem; where we don't want to declare that things are now beyond us; where we don't want to acknowledge that we are at our wit's end. Ultimately, we escape in denial.

Nothing passes a time more sweetly than a gossip. It makes us feel better at the cost of putting another down. Many will not out-rightly put others down in action, but their conversations in gossip are always putting them down. Gossiping is talking about others in a way that makes the talker feel better about themselves.

There are many other "escapes" and if you find that you are consciously or unconsciously engaging in any of the mentioned ones or the ones that cross your mind, there's much more work to be done on your healing and growth, sobriety and recovery.

ABOUT BEING DESPERATE:

Things get hard when you are desperate. When you lose that desperation, they become easy. The Lord is my Shepherd, I shall not want (I shall not be desperate).

One of the things God works on in recovery is to purge desperation.

Desperation can drive you nuts. You hit walls. It's possible to pursue something relentlessly without being desperate and only God can give you that.

Desperation keeps us in toxic relationships. Desperation keeps us from working on ourselves. Desperation always looks for shortcuts. Desperation makes us sly, deceptive, manipulative and controlling.

Desperation got some of us lying about our sobriety when we slip that we may keep our jobs, or maintain that status quo our "sobriety" got us.

Desperation has got some to seek out unconventional means of finding sobriety for instance; flying their loved ones abroad, or locking them up or getting them imprisoned and so much more.

Desperation got many trusting people that will not help their loved ones heal and grow. Addiction is unlike any other thing out there. The most skilled of people at solving many of life's complicated problems might fail when it comes to addiction. Desperation blinds our eyes to this.

Being desperate gets many of us doing things we don't like to pose as if we are working on our recovery, sobriety ... Yet there are things we can do that we like (and grow in them) that will help us heal and grow.

In the view of the fact that we are desperate to show the world we are working on us, we embrace a lot of things that are not us- and later we wonder why we aren't satisfied in our recovery.

To maintain lasting sobriety, we have to not be desperate. Let's talk about that.

When you look at points in your recovery where you relapsed or almost relapsed, there was some kind of desperation at play. When we are desperate for validation, at times this leads to a relapse where we seek validation from the wrong people- in this case, our old drinking buddies.

Being desperate is very different from hungering for something. Being desperate means that you are willing to compromise who you are to get what you want and hungering for something means that, yes, you want it but are willing to wait to get it without compromising who you are.

Some are so desperate to get sober that they run to science to alter their biochemistry not to desire alcohol or substances physically. These shortcuts always have consequences, most especially when it comes to manipulating neurotransmitters and the biochemistry of the body. Science is desperate to come up with a "pill" to fix addiction. They have tried in vain.

Hitting rock bottom deflates the ego and empties the tanks of being desperate. When a person is desperate, they will manipulate things to get what they want. Hitting rock bottom is realizing that there's nothing more to manipulate or to control to get what you are desperate for anymore. The tank is empty.

In recovery, what works is hunger, not being desperate. Hitting rock bottom lights up the flame of hunger. Being desperate comes from the ego while hunger comes from the spirit.

A person who is desperate can take on whatever comes their way that may "solve" their need but a person who is hungry is very selective about what they take on and only choose the best.

Being desperate comes from the ego or is a yearning of the ego while hunger is the yearning of the spirit. They look and feel similar in a way but when a line is drawn, you can clearly tell the difference.

Being desperate breaks but hunger builds. For instance, when one is desperate for intimacy, they will seek a way to find it anywhere with anyone. But when a person is hungry for intimacy, they will wait, keep themselves pure and be intimate with the right one. The same works for recovery.

So how do we hunger and shift from being desperate in our recovery?

The first thing we have to do is pray for the grace to wait, to be patient. We have been used for quite a while to get things done our way, to have our own way and get what we want. One common trait among all those who struggle with addiction is impatience. Being patient and always praying for the grace to be patient is one.

Secondly, being humble (praying for the grace to be humble). Another trait that is common with people struggling with addiction is pride. Pride fans the ego (manipulation and control). When humility comes into the picture, being desperate flies out and gives room to hunger.

Third, becoming honest (praying for the grace to be honest). Deceit, lies and secrecy fuel being desperate. When honesty is fronted in situations, room is given to hunger.

Selfishness is very common among those struggling with addiction. We become desperate when we want something for ourselves, to meet our needs and to maintain our interests. In becoming selfless (praying for the grace to be selfless), room is given to hunger.

A person who is hungry will seek out things about recovery, will read literature, will watch films, documentaries ... and put an effort in gaining wisdom.

A person who is hungry will move slow in stepping forward. His or her focus will be in going deeper (wisdom and knowledge) or rising higher (by dropping weights and letting go that has been holding that person down).

There's movement but it's not forward. It's progress on the vertical axis. The most interesting thing is with things spirit that as you rise higher, you simultaneously go deeper. Letting go graces you with more depth and more wisdom (deeper).

A person who is hungry will enjoy perfect solitude. Remember being desperate seeks validation or escapes. Perfect solitude is being peaceful when one is by themselves. Hunger pushes one to spend more time meditating and improving their relationship with God.

Matthew 5:6 AMPC

Blessed and fortunate and happy and spiritually prosperous (in that state in which the born-again child of God enjoys His favor and salvation) are those who **hunger** and thirst for righteousness (uprightness and right standing with God), for they shall be completely satisfied! [Isa. 55:1, 2.]

When we see hunger in this way, this verse makes so much sense.

For they shall be completely satisfied ... They shall not be desperate for anything.

To fully recover, be hungry. Don't be desperate.

DOING THE GOOD I OUGHT TO DO:

Romans 7:15 New International Version

I do not understand what I do. For what I want to do I do not do, but what I hate I do.

Let's talk about the three stages of recovery under the guidance of this verse.

The first stage is the stage of wanting, desiring to do what you "hate to do." Here is where you give in to what you know is pulling you down but you enjoy the ride. Here is where it gives you the thrill, the adrenalin rush, the beautiful way of escape, the temporary happiness.

This is a stage of denial, of delusion, of false hope and comfort, pride ... We all go through this stage in our recovery. It's a caterpillar stage where we are very destructive, careless and loose. Where the sin in us (sin can be defined as the unhealthy patterns or behaviors, unhealthy ways of coping we have picked up along the way in our lives) pushes us to do what we "hate to do."

The second stage is "having no desire or yearning to do what you "hate" to do anymore but you still do it." This is a stage of acceptance, humility, conviction and an admission of powerlessness. Conviction kicks in and we desire to set our feet on a different path but we are powerless over it. This is where the split in our souls becomes obvious. A part of us wants the change so bad and another desires the comfort of complacency.

The third stage of recovery is "not doing what you hate to do anymore and having power over it." In our case, that's staying sober.

The third stage is where God takes over. Where He empowers you to do what you ought to do and gives you the grace (power over) of not doing what you don't want to do. This is the stage of absolute sobriety for us. This is the stage of no resistance for us- where we don't have to fight with cravings or urges. This is the stage where we are sober regardless of what is happening in our lives.

Most of us struggle in the second stage. Shining a light into it can help us heal. Doing an inventory helps. Doing what you ought not to do can at times be a very sweet escape. What unhealthy coping mechanisms are favoring that sweet escape in you? Light that exposes these things even on the level of the mind is still powerful to bring about change.

ADDRESSING ADDICTION AT THE WORKPLACE:

These are the mechanisms of addressing addiction in the workplace.

Majorly, this is more about overcoming triggers at the workplace. Knowing what the triggers are at the workplace and finding ways round them or through them is key. What are the triggers in the workplace or work environment?

Here is a list of some of the triggers at the workplace. The list is not exhaustive because I'm typing it as it comes to me. You can add more to it.

- Beating deadlines.
- Keeping up appearances.
- Peer influence.
- Unrealistic demands.
- Shady deals, conspiracies.
- Unresolved home issues that overflow into work.
- Tension from unresolved issues with workmates.
- Delay in delivery.
- Secrecy (a person struggling with a habit hiding it)

- Guilt that arises from 9.

- Competition, workmates rivalry.

- Kindly add more ...

When it comes to beating deadlines, the core values of honesty and integrity come into play. Don't take on something you can't handle or that you can't be able to accomplish before the deadline. It's from taking on things like that that we put ourselves under much pressure which hurls us deeper into dark pits of not necessarily addiction but guilt and fear.

Be honest about what you can take on. Although the lure is appealing, don't give in to it. One of the things recovery makes us aware of is what we are capable of taking on. Learning to say "no" to some things not only gives you peace but builds your self-esteem.

- Recovery teaches us to be ourselves. When you are comfortable with who you are (recognizing and appreciating your growth), you can't be moved by what others do. You are comfortable with packing your own food and not eating at that fancy restaurant workmates eat from. You are comfortable with doing you and not doing anything outside you. You are comfortable with your weird.

Keeping up appearances is rooted in deception. The less the deception in one's life, the more the peace. Much of the pressure that's in the workplace doesn't arise from the actual work but keeping up appearances.

- Addressing peer influence: Discovering who you are is an indirect reward of persistently keeping on the path of recovery. As you grow in Step 11, you will grow/become aware/discover/love/appreciate/enjoy/be peaceful about who you are. Struggling to impress will not be a bother to you. You rise from the plane of doing things because of influence, to doing things because of choice.

- When it comes to unrealistic demands made by, for instance bosses (I've heard many suffer in this area where bosses make sexual demands), again learning to say no helps. Refusing such is rooted in your self-esteem.

Recovery teaches us that we would rather lose anything than our sobriety and all that comes along with it like an improved self-esteem. Keeping a job while feeling like trash at that job is not worth it.

- When it comes to doing shady deals and handling conspiracies in the workplace, we ask ourselves- what does recovery enlighten us to do in such situations? Recovery enlightens us to honesty. Recovery enlightens us to being street smart. Being street smart is knowing that all that is hidden will be exposed and it always comes back to the one who does it. It may come back in waves of guilt, or a spoilt reputation. Is that worth your recovery?

- About unresolved home issues that overflow into work we ask ourselves, have we made amends? Have we drawn healthy boundaries? Are we living honest and being accountable? When a husband is new to recovery and working late, the wife will suspect something is happening- are you working on better communication to lessen the suspicion?

- When it comes to tension with workmates, we ask ourselves some questions. We do an inventory. Are we sending mixed signals to workmates or are being clear in our communication? Do we keep our boundaries professional and if we cross the line, are we ready to carry that cross in purity with whoever we are crossing that line with? Are we being responsible and ready to carry the weight of our mistakes?

- Delay in delivery takes us back to being honest about what we can take on. You can't take it all on. When you find what you can take on that's in your docket, you will discover that you can take on much more if you say no to taking on to what's not in your docket. Eat what you can.

- Hiding our habits arises from the stigma. Being open about who you are and what you are struggling with is key in this. You have much more to lose if you keep on hiding who you are and what you are struggling with. That's peace of mind! And in business/workplace terms, losing peace of mind is translated into low efficiency, little return on investment, unimpressive presentations unmoving, uninspired, etc. Hiding who you are is counterproductive and recovery makes us aware of that.

If your work rejects who you are, they are not worth you.

There's not feeling appreciated because of feelings of inferiority on your part (a low self-esteem) and there's not feeling appreciated because even when you have worked on you and don't have issues with your esteem, some will still not appreciate you. This is the kind of not being (not feeling) appreciated that you should walk away from whether in a workplace environment or a friendship …

When it comes to competition and rivalry, recovery awakens us to the truth that everyone has his or her own race. The blessing is not in what you do. The blessing is in discovering who you are and recovery sets us on that path. No one, and nothing can dim your shine when you have set your eyes upon healing and growth. Things don't happen to you. They happen for you when you are intentional about your healing and growth.

This is all I can share today. I don't prepare but type as I'm inspired. I may not have touched all the scenarios in the workplace environment but I hope this helps.

TOOLS OF OVERCOMING ADDICTION:

When we say the "tools to overcome addiction," we mean "what we need to stay sober," or "what we have to have to stay sober." The "tools" are emotional and spiritual in nature. I'm going to go through some tools I have thought of that will help.

- **Unlearning unhealthy coping mechanisms.** In our lives, we have gone through trauma and have encountered harsh emotional environments. Along the way, we have picked up survival skills that are very toxic like lying and being deceptive. We have found ways to cope that are unhealthy.

Identifying these unhealthy coping mechanisms and then putting in effort to unlearn them is key that will help one stay sober.

- **Dealing with guilt.** Guilt is one of the strongest emotions that drives us deeper into pits of addiction. Embracing healthy ways to deal with guilt like making amends, coming clean, being accountable and acceptance of full responsibility of our actions helps to deal with guilt.

- **ND deal with fear.** Pride arises to protect fear. Fear expresses itself in many dimensions, for instance inferiority complexes, superiority complexes, feelings of inadequacy, feelings of being better than others. When healthy ways are embraced to deal with fear, a person will easily maintain sobriety. What are some of these ways? Growing in faith- working the program, doing the next right thing out of faith.

- **Changing one's view about who God is.** People struggling with addiction are always in a "flight" mode. Running away from a God they perceive is a punisher and tough judge that wants to penalize. In recovery, we get to learn that God is a very merciful God, and gracious. He forgives anything when we run to Him in repentance and in His mercy, He gives us not what we deserve. Changing how we see God can help us stay sober.

- **Dealing with past pain and trauma.** Past pain and trauma puts us in flight mode, either consciously or unconsciously. We run to things that can ease our discomfort, and in the run, we get hooked to either unhealthy behaviors or substances. Recovery teaches us to face our pain and trauma and also identifying it, for example in doing an inventory.

- **Another tool is learning how to Pray- depending on God.** In active addiction, we depended on ourselves, our will, what we knew, who we knew, our influence etc. In recovery, we learn to put that all aside and depend on God. This is one way of exercising humility, that in even the smallest of things, we ask God to reveal His will to us.

- **Expand your knowledge base.** Knowledge is power. Get as much information as you can about recovery. Get to know about psychology, get as much knowledge as you can about spiritual principles like grace, mercy. Befriend those that know more or are more experienced in recovery than you and always consult with them. Expand your knowledge base.

•	**Grow in hope.** A person who is struggling with something always struggles with despair. Growing in hope is key. How does a person grow in hope? Your hope is emptied every time you run to that substance of choice for peace. The first step in growing in hope is staying sober. The second step is making moves under the lead of the 12 steps. In progressing along that path, hope grows.

•	**Grow in solitude.** Learn to spend time alone with yourself and God. Pray and meditate. Alcohol, drugs, gambling and other addictions are mostly escapes. We engage in them because we are running away from either being lonely or bored. Prayer and meditation help in this respect. improving our conscious contact with God. You can do this seated with a pen and paper and let inspiration flow.

An indirect result of solitude is finding meaning in everything which kindles purpose.

•	**Another tool is service.** Do something outside yourself for another regularly. People who struggle with addiction are selfish in nature. When you do something outside yourself daily, for another, you come against that selfishness (which lurks at the root of addiction). Do things that counter selfishness, pride, deception and grow in recovery.

- **Sanctify or separate yourself.** A person in recovery is a special person. Even in active addiction, we saw that we never could fully fit in. When we walk into recovery, we realize that we can't do things the way everyone does them. We find that we may have to find new friends and let go of our old friends. That's a process of separation. We find that we have to spend a lot of time alone to ourselves and God.

- **Dealing with pride.** Pride manifests in many ways. Pride always comes before a fall. If you want to grow or rise in recovery, humility is key. God exalts the humble. Humility is stopping to blame others and finding fault with oneself. Instead of saying that they did me wrong, we ask, "what did I do wrong?" As a person grows in humility, God exalts them, that is to say, He helps them stay sober in instances where they normally wouldn't stay sober.

- **Confide in someone.** To walk this journey, you have to have someone that you confide in. Liverpool has a very good motto- "You'll never walk alone." I don't follow football but I marked that. And indeed, you'll never walk alone in the recovery journey. There's power, wisdom, encouragement, a different way of seeing things in fellowship.

These are some of the tools I have thought of to overcome addiction.

ABOUT CONFIDENTIALITY:

To me, confidentiality means the ability to keep a secret, to hang onto exclusive information and not spread it, to stay composed when you find out something. In service work, we have access to exclusive information.

And it also means a deep understanding of the times we are in.

2 Timothy 3:1-5 NIV

But mark this: There will be terrible times in the last days. People will be lovers of themselves, lovers of money, boastful, proud, abusive, disobedient to their parents, ungrateful, unholy, without love, unforgiving, slanderous, without self-control, brutal, not lovers of the good, treacherous, rash, conceited, lovers of pleasure rather than lovers of God— having a form of godliness but denying its power. Have nothing to do with such people.

What these verses are saying is, people will do weird things, unbelievable things. People will hide deep secrets. There will be deep betrayals. People will go great extents to hide darkness. People will do weird things to cope. Very few people are straight in their paths. There's a lot of darkness in us.

The most sensible of people will do the weirdest of things. The person you think is very straight could be the most crooked. Confidentiality to me means, even when you find this out, you stay composed.

We are as sick as our secrets, and a person that's in service especially to pass on healing to the next, should front confidentiality. There are people who have no history with addiction or anything, but because of that one thing they did, they are in much guilt. That drives them deeper into addiction.

To cope, people do all kinds of things. A person who is mature is nonjudgmental in his or her approach in helping others. I believe that is why God uses people who have gone through something to help others when they have worked on themselves to heal because a big secret rarely moves them. Those who are forgiven much love much.

Luke 7:47-48 NIV

Therefore, I tell you, her many sins have been forgiven—as her great love

(maturity, patience, compassion, empathy, tolerance, being nonjudgmental …) has shown. But whoever has been forgiven little loves little (is impatient, intolerant, immature, judgmental …)." Then Jesus said to her, "Your sins are forgiven."

I'm not adding to the Lord's word but helping us understand it better, deeper with more clarification. With this deeper understanding, you will find that the Bible is the best Mental Health Manual ever written.

There's a lot happening in the field of recovery where people are breaching confidentiality to make money but it shouldn't be that way. Maturity is saying no and standing by it.

The right way of helping a person heal and grow is to guide them to a point of growth that they may be able to tell it themselves and, in the process, helping them also to build the capacity to bear the consequences or the reward of telling it. At times, the reward of coming out might break them if they haven't built the capacity to handle it. Or the consequence.

A secret is very heavy upon the bearer. Knowing this should inspire whoever has positioned themselves to help to keep confidentiality.

Some are struggling with abuse, others are struggling with their sexuality, some have done outrageous things. Thing is, we have all sinned and fallen short. Some have stolen, lied, cheated … and guilt is eating them away. Some have compromised a lot to rise in corporate ranks, some are hiding their real jobs from their families (many are involved in trafficking if some kind), most especially sex trafficking. There's a lot happening. People have very dark secrets. Some are sleeping with their relatives. Maturity in recovery means that when a person comes out or opens up to you, you maintain your composure.

Some are hiding secret envies that are eating them away. We all need someone to talk to and unload. Someone mature. Someone we can confide in.

This is all I can say about confidentiality. It's keeping one's composure when one gets exclusive info. The media hasn't even tapped into 1 percent of what is happening. There's much that is not being told. Why? There are few mature enough to handle it.

Confidentiality is the skill of being able to keep a secret and in recovery, it goes a step further! It's the wisdom, guidance, inspiration, depth to help the bearer of the secret build capacity to tell that secret themselves with no reservations whatsoever. It's from that that true healing flows.

ABOUT EX-LOVERS:

When it comes to ex-lovers, there's work that needs to be done in us more especially from our side. There are certain moves we ought to make, certain pieces we have to pick up and straighten, a couple of things we have to let go of and identify codependency.

The first step to me is identifying what need (yours) ex-lovers where helping you to meet. If a healthy replacement for that need has not yet been found, you will find that they will always trigger you in certain situations.

Identifying these needs comes with a lot of work on your self-esteem, that determines your sense of worth. It has more to do with you and the effort you are putting in to heal and grow than on them.

The first need ex-lovers help us meet is intimacy. Now this might not be exactly physical but just the thought of it. When a person in recovery has not found a healthy replacement to meet that need, ex-lovers will always trigger you. Replacements like pornography, flirting …, being loose will always leave the door open for ex-lovers to trigger a person in recovery.

A healthy replacement can be abstinence. Abstinence can mean one or two things. The first is restraining your sexual energy. This is vain and a person in recovery will always fail if they restrain their sexual energy. It is one of the strongest forces of nature. Like I said in the beginning, it doesn't have to be physical.

The second meaning of abstinence is converting that sexual energy into something else. Sublimation. This is work you have to do and ask yourself in what healthy ways can you convert your sexual energy?

Another healthy replacement is commitment. Loyalty to one person.

The second need ex-lovers help us meet is money (or in emotional terms, security). A person in recovery has to find a healthy replacement for that. When you get a sense of security from another, you leave the door wide open for manipulation and control. You should get that sense of security from God, not a person. There's work that needs to be done so that God is solely the one you depend on for security.

You ask, how does that relate to my finances. God is the source of ideas, favor, wisdom, strategy (we see this in the Old Testament where he gave strategy to kings to defeat their enemies). He gives business strategies today.

God will do one or two things when it comes to your finances. He will either position you in service, where He provides for you by prompting others to give to you. This is in cases where your service is of benefit to many.

Or he will give you an idea. Like opening up a LinkedIn or Xing, or reviewing your CV.

So that you depend on not a person but Him for security, in this case, financial.

The second need ex-lovers help us meet is the need to be with someone. To deal with the discomfort of being lonely or bored. Again, work has to be done by a person in recovery to find healthy replacements for this, other than people.

In my experience, whenever I tried to fill that space of being lonely or bored with someone, I always ended up with someone more toxic. I don't know if this is the case with most of us. I am very conscious and aware that whenever I run to a person to ease the discomfort of being bored or lonely, I always hit walls.

Peace in solitude is one of the long-term rewards recovery avails to us. We don't need to escape.

Work has to be put in to be at peace in solitude. Any behavior or pattern you pick up to deal with loneliness or boredom will ultimately turn toxic; even if it is very good. Dealing with this the best way is by doing Step 11.

Step 11. Sought through prayer and meditation to improve our conscious contact with God as we understood Him, praying only for knowledge of His will for us and the power to carry that out.

When Step 11 is done, The Lord becomes your Shepard and you shall not want (be desperate for anything to ease your discomfort of being lonely or bored).

The other need ex-lovers help us meet is the need of having someone to talk to.

There are many examples of this in the Bible. The relationship of Jonathan and David is an imagery of the relationship we are supposed to have with God.

Whenever you are desperate to have someone to talk to, you are opening up doors to be manipulated and controlled. There's choosing to talk to someone and being desperate to talk to someone. It's the desperation with the issue, not the talking to someone. Work has to be put in. That desperation should be first channeled toward God. Whenever you feel like telling someone something, first tell it to God.

In the beginning, it will not make sense. As you go on, God becomes that Friend who sticks closer than a brother. Just keep at it. Many of the spiritual things rarely make sense in the beginning but when we are consistent, they grow on us and make sense.

After identifying the needs ex-lovers help one in recovery meet and finding healthy replacements for them, we go on to identify the resentments we have against ex-lovers.

Is there some kind of unforgiveness when it comes to this ex-lover? Bitterness or hatred or anger? Again, these things open up doors in us to be triggered, manipulated and controlled either by them or by another that fills their shoes- the size is always the same or smaller (more toxic)!

Letting go, forgiving, getting closure ..., is the way to go in this.

Then, lastly, drawing healthy boundaries.

Confiding in God, getting close to God that He becomes that friend who sticks closer than a brother helps much in drawing healthy boundaries. A thing that plays behind the scenes is that when a person is hurting, they will always confide in the "wrong" person. Why? Because their emotional compass is broken.

Drawing healthy boundaries like meeting them and have a healthy break off with them. Not cutting them off just like that.

Those who are blocked and ghosted always return and they always trigger. But those who ties are cut off respectfully (on your part) lose their power to trigger you.

There are many instances where healthy boundaries can be drawn. Like avoiding late night talks. Not going to certain places among many.

ABOUT THE AUTHOR

Michael Gabriel Kintu Kayondo

Was Addicted — Jesus Set Me Free — Shining Recovery